U.S. Department
of Transportation

**Federal Aviation
Administration**

FAA-S-ACS-8B

I0087457

Instrument Rating – Airplane
Airman Certification Standards

June 2018

**Flight Standards Service
Washington, DC 20591**

Acknowledgments

The U.S. Department of Transportation, Federal Aviation Administration (FAA), Office of Safety Standards, Regulatory Support Division, Airman Testing Branch, P.O. Box 25082, Oklahoma City, OK 73125 developed this Airman Certification Standards (ACS) document with the assistance of the aviation community. The FAA gratefully acknowledges the valuable support from the many individuals and organizations who contributed their time and expertise to assist in this endeavor.

Availability

This ACS is available for download from www.faa.gov. Please send comments regarding this document the Airman Testing Branch Mailbox using the email: afs630comments@faa.gov.

Material in FAA-S-ACS-8B will be effective June 11, 2018. All previous editions of the Instrument Rating – Airplane Airman Certification Standards will be obsolete as of this date for airplane applicants.

Foreword

The Federal Aviation Administration (FAA) has published the Instrument Rating – Airplane Airman Certification Standards (ACS) document to communicate the aeronautical knowledge, risk management, and flight proficiency standards for the instrument rating in the airplane category, single-engine land and sea; and multiengine land and sea classes. This ACS incorporates and supersedes FAA-S-ACS-8A Instrument Rating – Airplane Airman Certification Standards.

The FAA views the ACS as the foundation of its transition to a more integrated and systematic approach to airman certification. The ACS is part of the Safety Management System (SMS) framework that the FAA uses to mitigate risks associated with airman certification training and testing. Specifically, the ACS, associated guidance, and test question components of the airman certification system are constructed around the four functional components of an SMS:

- Safety Policy that defines and describes aeronautical knowledge, flight proficiency, and risk management as integrated components of the airman certification system;

- Safety Risk Management processes through which internal and external stakeholders identify and evaluate regulatory changes, safety recommendations, and other factors that require modification of airman testing and training materials;

- Safety Assurance processes to ensure the prompt and appropriate incorporation of changes arising from new regulations and safety recommendations; and

- Safety Promotion in the form of ongoing engagement with both external stakeholders (e.g., the aviation training industry) and FAA policy divisions.

The FAA has developed this ACS and its associated guidance in collaboration with a diverse group of aviation training experts. The goal is to drive a systematic approach to all components of the airman certification system, including knowledge test question development and conduct of the practical test. The FAA acknowledges and appreciates the many hours that these aviation experts have contributed toward this goal. This level of collaboration, a hallmark of a robust safety culture, strengthens and enhances aviation safety at every level of the airman certification system.

John S. Duncan
Executive Director, Flight Standards Service

Revision History

Document #	Description	Revision Date
FAA-S-8081-4E	Instrument Rating for Airplane, Practical Test Standards (with Changes 1-5)	January 2010
FAA-S-ACS-8	Instrument Rating Airplane Airman Certification Standards	June 1, 2016
FAA-S-ACS-8	Instrument Rating Airplane Airman Certification Standards (Change 1)	June 15, 2016
FAA-S-ACS-8A	Instrument Rating – Airplane Airman Certification Standards	June 12, 2017
FAA-S-ACS-8B	Instrument Rating – Airplane Airman Certification Standards	June 11, 2018

Major Enhancements to Version FAA-S-ACS-8B

- Revised references to reflect FAA reorganization.
- Added language to account for Part 68 BasicMed.
- Added "solely by reference to instruments" to applicable Task objectives.
- Reworded nonprecision approach Task elements to accommodate constant descent final approach (CDFA).
- Revised all Tasks in all Areas of Operation to include more standardized element order and element language.
- All applicants without a multiengine airplane center thrust limitation will now be required to supply an airplane with a published V_{MC} when accomplishing the test in a multiengine airplane.
- Updated the following Appendices:
  — Appendix 1: The Knowledge Test Eligibility, Prerequisites, and Testing Centers.
  — Appendix 3: Airman Knowledge Test Report
  — Appendix 4: The Practical Test – Eligibility and Prerequisites
  — Appendix 5: Practical Test Roles, Responsibilities, and Outcomes.
  — Appendix 7: Aircraft, Equipment, and Operational Requirements & Limitations.
  — Appendix 8: Use of Flight Simulation Training Devices (FSTD) and Aviation Training Devices (ATD): Airplane Single-Engine, Multiengine Land and Sea
  — Appendix 9: References.
  — Appendix 10: Abbreviations and Acronyms.

Table of Contents

Introduction

Airman Certification Standards Concept

The goal of the airman certification process is to ensure the applicant possesses knowledge, ability to manage risks, and skill consistent with the privileges of the certificate or rating being exercised, in order to act as Pilot-in-Command (PIC).

In fulfilling its responsibilities for the airman certification process, the Federal Aviation Administration (FAA) Flight Standards Service (AFS) plans, develops, and maintains materials related to airman certification training and testing. These materials have included several components. The FAA knowledge test measures mastery of the aeronautical knowledge areas listed in Title 14 of the Code of Federal Regulations (14 CFR) part 61. Other materials, such as handbooks in the FAA-H-8083 series, provide guidance to applicants on aeronautical knowledge, risk management, and flight proficiency.

Safe operations in today's National Airspace System (NAS) require integration of aeronautical knowledge, risk management, and flight proficiency standards. To accomplish these goals, the FAA drew upon the expertise of organizations and individuals across the aviation and training community to develop the Airman Certification Standards (ACS). The ACS integrates the elements of knowledge, risk management, and skill listed in 14 CFR part 61 for each airman certificate or rating. It thus forms a more comprehensive standard for what an applicant must know, consider, and do for the safe conduct and successful completion of each Task to be tested on both the qualifying FAA knowledge test and the oral and flight portions of the practical test.

During the ground and flight portion of the practical test, the FAA expects evaluators to assess the applicant's mastery of the topic in accordance with the level of learning most appropriate for the specified Task. The oral questioning will continue throughout the entire practical test. For some topics, the evaluator will ask the applicant to describe or explain. For other items, the evaluator will assess the applicant's understanding by providing a scenario that requires the applicant to appropriately apply and/or correlate knowledge, experience, and information to the circumstances of the given scenario. The flight portion of the practical test requires the applicant to demonstrate knowledge, risk management, flight proficiency, and operational skill in accordance with the ACS.

Note: *As used in the ACS, an evaluator is any person authorized to conduct airman testing (e.g., an FAA Aviation Safety Inspector (ASI), Designated Pilot Examiner (DPE), or other individual authorized to conduct a test for a certificate or rating.)*

Using the ACS

The ACS consists of **Areas of Operation** arranged in a logical sequence, beginning with Preflight Preparation and ending with Postflight Procedures. Each Area of Operation includes **Tasks** appropriate to that Area of Operation. Each Task begins with an **Objective** stating what the applicant should know, consider, and/or do. The ACS then lists the aeronautical knowledge, risk management, and skill elements relevant to the specific Task, along with the conditions and standards for acceptable performance. The ACS uses **Notes** to emphasize special considerations. The ACS uses the terms "will" and "must" to convey directive (mandatory) information. The term "may" denotes items that are recommended but not required. The **References** for each Task indicate the source material for Task elements. For example, in Tasks such as "Current and forecast weather for departure, arrival, and en route phases of flight" (IR.I.B.K1), the applicant should be prepared for questions on any weather product presented in the references for that Task.

The abbreviation(s) within parentheses immediately following a Task refer to the category and/or class airplane appropriate to that Task. The meaning of each abbreviation is as follows:

ASEL: Airplane – Single-Engine Land
ASES: Airplane – Single-Engine Sea
AMEL: Airplane – Multiengine Land
AMES: Airplane – Multiengine Sea

Note: *When administering a test based on this ACS, the Tasks appropriate to the class airplane (ASEL, ASES, AMEL, or AMES) used for the test must be included in the plan of action. The absence of a class indicates the Task is for all classes.*

Each Task in the ACS is coded according to a scheme that includes four elements. For example:

IR.I.C.K4:

- **IR** = Applicable ACS (Instrument Rating – Airplane)
- **I** = Area of Operation (Preflight Preparation)
- **C** = Task (Cross-Country Flight Planning)
- **K4** = Task Element Knowledge 4 (Elements of an IFR flight plan.)

Knowledge test questions are linked to the ACS codes, which will ultimately replace the system of Learning Statement Codes (LSC). After this transition occurs, the Airman Knowledge Test Report (AKTR) will list an ACS code that correlates to a specific Task element for a given Area of Operation and Task. Remedial instruction and re-testing will be specific, targeted, and based on specified learning criteria. Similarly, a Notice of Disapproval for the practical test will use the ACS codes to identify the deficient Task elements.

The current knowledge test management system does not have the capability to print ACS codes. Until a new test management system is in place, the LSC (e.g., "PLT058") code will continue to be displayed on the AKTR. The LSC codes are linked to references leading to broad subject areas. By contrast, each ACS code is tied to a unique Task element in the ACS itself. Because of this fundamental difference, there is no one-to-one correlation between LSC codes and ACS codes.

Because all active knowledge test questions for the Instrument Rating Airplane (IRA) knowledge test have been aligned with the corresponding ACS, evaluators can continue to use LSC codes in conjunction with the ACS for the time being. The evaluator should look up the LSC code(s) on the applicant's AKTR in the Learning Statement Reference Guide available using the following link: https://www.faa.gov/training_testing/testing/media/ LearningStatementReferenceGuide.pdf. After noting the subject area(s), the evaluator can use the corresponding Area(s) of Operation/Task(s) in the ACS to narrow the scope of material for retesting, and to evaluate the applicant's understanding of that material in the context of the appropriate ACS Area(s) of Operation and Task(s).

Applicants for a combined Private Pilot Certificate with Instrument Rating, in accordance with 14 CFR part 61, section 61.65 (a) and (g), must pass all areas designated in the Private Pilot Airplane (PAR) ACS and the Instrument Rating Airplane (IRA) ACS. Examiners need not duplicate Tasks. For example, only one preflight demonstration would be required; however, the Preflight Task from the IRA ACS would be more extensive than the Preflight Task from the PAR ACS to ensure readiness for Instrument Flight Rules (IFR) flight.

A combined certificate and rating evaluation should be treated as one practical test, requiring only one application and resulting in only one temporary certificate, disapproval notice, or letter of discontinuance, as applicable. Failure of any Task will result in a failure of the entire test and application. Therefore, even if the deficient maneuver was instrument related and the performance of all visual flight rules (VFR) Tasks was determined to be satisfactory, the applicant will receive a notice of disapproval.

The applicant must pass the IRA knowledge test before taking the instrument rating practical test. The practical test is conducted in accordance with the ACS that is current as of the date of the test. Further, the applicant must pass the ground portion of the practical test before beginning the flight portion.

The ground portion of the practical test allows the evaluator to determine whether the applicant is sufficiently prepared to advance to the flight portion of the practical test. The oral questioning will continue throughout the entire practical test.

The FAA encourages applicants and instructors to use the ACS when preparing for knowledge tests and practical tests. The FAA will revise the ACS as circumstances require.

I. Preflight Preparation

Task	A. *Pilot Qualifications*
References	14 CFR part 61; FAA-H-8083-2, FAA-H-8083-15, AC 68-1
Objective	To determine the applicant exhibits satisfactory knowledge, risk management, and skills associated with the requirements to act as PIC under instrument flight rules.
Knowledge	The applicant demonstrates understanding of:
IR.I.A.K1	Certification requirements, recency of experience, and record keeping.
IR.I.A.K2	Privileges and limitations.
IR.I.A.K3	Part 68 BasicMed Privileges and Limitations.
Risk Management	The applicant demonstrates the ability to identify, assess and mitigate risks, encompassing:
IR.I.A.R1	Failure to distinguish proficiency versus currency.
IR.I.A.R2	Failure to set personal minimums.
IR.I.A.R3	Failure to ensure fitness for flight and physiological factors that might affect the pilot's ability to fly under instrument conditions.
IR.I.A.R4	Flying unfamiliar airplanes, or operating with unfamiliar flight display systems and avionics.
Skills	The applicant demonstrates the ability to:
IR.I.A.S1	Apply requirements to act as PIC under Instrument Flight Rules (IFR) in a scenario given by the evaluator.

I. Preflight Preparation

Task	B. *Weather Information*
References	14 CFR part 91; FAA-H-8083-25, AC 00-6; AC 00-45, AIM
Objective	To determine the applicant exhibits satisfactory knowledge, risk management, and skills associated with obtaining, understanding, and applying weather information for a flight under IFR.
Knowledge	The applicant demonstrates understanding of:
IR.I.B.K1	Acceptable sources of weather data for flight planning purposes.
IR.I.B.K2	Weather products and resources utilized for preflight planning, current and forecast weather for departure and en route operations and arrival phases of flight.
IR.I.B.K3	Meteorology applicable to the departure, en route, alternate, and destination for flights conducted under IFR in Instrument Meteorological Conditions (IMC) to include expected climate and hazardous conditions such as:
IR.I.B.K3a	a. Atmospheric composition and stability
IR.I.B.K3b	b. Wind (e.g. crosswind, tailwind, windshear, etc.)
IR.I.B.K3c	c. Temperature
IR.I.B.K3d	d. Moisture/precipitation
IR.I.B.K3e	e. Weather system formation, including air masses and fronts
IR.I.B.K3f	f. Clouds
IR.I.B.K3g	g. Turbulence
IR.I.B.K3h	h. Thunderstorms and microbursts
IR.I.B.K3i	i. Icing and freezing level information
IR.I.B.K3j	j. Fog
IR.I.B.K3k	k. Frost
IR.I.B.K4	Flight deck displays of digital weather and aeronautical information.
Risk Management	The applicant demonstrates the ability to identify, assess and mitigate risks, encompassing:
IR.I.B.R1	Factors involved in making the go/no-go and continue/divert decisions, to include:
IR.I.B.R1a	a. Circumstances that would make diversion prudent
IR.I.B.R1b	b. Personal Weather Minimums
IR.I.B.R1c	c. Hazardous weather conditions to include known or forecast icing or turbulence aloft
IR.I.B.R2	Limitations of:
IR.I.B.R2a	a. Onboard weather equipment
IR.I.B.R2b	b. Aviation weather reports and forecasts
IR.I.B.R2c	c. Inflight weather resources
Skills	The applicant demonstrates the ability to:
IR.I.B.S1	Use available aviation weather resources to obtain an adequate weather briefing.
IR.I.B.S2	Discuss the implications of at least three of the conditions listed in K3a through K3k above, using actual weather or weather conditions in a scenario provided by the evaluator.
IR.I.B.S3	Correlate weather information to make a competent go/no-go decision.
IR.I.B.S4	Determine whether an alternate airport is required, and, if required, whether the selected alternate airport meets regulatory requirements.

I. Preflight Preparation

Task	C. Cross-Country Flight Planning
References	14 CFR part 91; FAA-H-8083-2, FAA-H-8083-15, FAA-H-8083-16, FAA-H-8083-25; Navigation Charts, Chart Supplements; AIM; NOTAMs
Objective	To determine the applicant exhibits satisfactory knowledge, risk management, and skills associated with planning an IFR cross-country and filing an IFR flight plan.
Knowledge	The applicant demonstrates understanding of:
IR.I.C.K1	Route planning, including consideration of the available navigational facilities, special use airspace, preferred routes, and alternate airports.
IR.I.C.K2	Altitude selection accounting for terrain and obstacles, glide distance of airplane, IFR cruising altitudes, effect of wind, and oxygen requirements.
IR.I.C.K3	Calculating:
IR.I.C.K3a	a. Time, climb and descent rates, course, distance, heading, true airspeed, and groundspeed
IR.I.C.K3b	b. Estimated time of arrival to include conversion to universal coordinated time (UTC)
IR.I.C.K3c	c. Fuel requirements, to include reserve
IR.I.C.K4	Elements of an IFR flight plan.
IR.I.C.K5	Procedures for activating and closing an IFR flight plan in controlled and uncontrolled airspace.
Risk Management	The applicant demonstrates the ability to identify, assess and mitigate risks, encompassing:
IR.I.C.R1	Pilot.
IR.I.C.R2	Airplane.
IR.I.C.R3	Environment (e.g., weather, airports, airspace, terrain, obstacles).
IR.I.C.R4	External pressures.
IR.I.C.R5	Limitations of air traffic control (ATC) services.
IR.I.C.R6	Limitations of electronic planning applications and programs.
IR.I.C.R7	Improper fuel planning.
Skills	The applicant demonstrates the ability to:
IR.I.C.S1	Prepare, present and explain a cross-country flight plan assigned by the evaluator including a risk analysis based on real time weather which includes calculating time en route and fuel considering factors such as power settings, operating altitude, wind, fuel reserve requirements, and weight and balance requirements.
IR.I.C.S2	Recalculate fuel reserves based on a scenario provided by the evaluator.
IR.I.C.S3	Create a navigation plan and simulate filing an IFR flight plan.
IR.I.C.S4	Interpret departure, arrival, en route, and approach procedures with reference to appropriate and current charts.
IR.I.C.S5	Recognize simulated wing contamination due to airframe icing and demonstrate knowledge of the adverse effects of airframe icing during pre-takeoff, takeoff, cruise, and landing phases of flight as well as the corrective actions.
IR.I.C.S6	Apply pertinent information from appropriate and current aeronautical charts, Charts Supplement; NOTAMs relative to airport, runway and taxiway closures; and other flight publications.

II. Preflight Procedures

Task	A. Airplane Systems Related to IFR Operations
References	14 CFR parts 61, 91; FAA-H-8083-2, FAA-H-8083-15; AFM; AC 91-74
Objective	To determine the applicant exhibits satisfactory knowledge, risk management, and skills associated with anti-icing and de-icing systems.
Knowledge	The applicant demonstrates understanding of:
IR.II.A.K1	The general operational characteristics and limitations of applicable anti-icing and deicing systems, including airframe, propeller, intake, fuel, and pitot-static systems.
Risk Management	The applicant demonstrates the ability to identify, assess and mitigate risks, encompassing:
IR.II.A.R1	Pilots with little or no experience with flight in icing conditions.
IR.II.A.R2	Limitations of anti-icing and deicing systems.
Skills	The applicant demonstrates the ability to:
IR.II.A.S1	Demonstrate familiarity with anti- or de-icing procedures and/or information published by the manufacturer that is specific to the airplane used on the practical test.

II. Preflight Procedures

Task	B. Airplane Flight Instruments and Navigation Equipment
References	14 CFR parts 61, 91; FAA-H-8083-15; AIM
Objective	To determine the applicant exhibits satisfactory knowledge, risk management, and skills associated with managing instruments appropriate for an IFR flight.
Knowledge	The applicant demonstrates understanding of:
IR.II.B.K1	Operation of their airplane's applicable flight instrument system(s) including:
IR.II.B.K1a	a. Pitot-static instrument system: altimeter, airspeed indicator, vertical speed indicator
IR.II.B.K1b	b. Gyroscopic/electric/vacuum instrument system: attitude indicator, heading indicator, turn-and-slip indicator/turn coordinator
IR.II.B.K1c	c. Electrical systems, electronic flight instrument displays (PFD, MFD), transponder
IR.II.B.K1d	d. Magnetic compass
IR.II.B.K2	Operation of their airplane's applicable navigation system(s) including:
IR.II.B.K2a	a. VOR, DME, ILS, marker beacon receiver/indicators
IR.II.B.K2b	b. RNAV, GPS, Wide Area Augmentation System (WAAS), FMS, autopilot
Risk Management	The applicant demonstrates the ability to identify, assess and mitigate risks, encompassing:
IR.II.B.R1	Failure to monitor and manage automated systems.
IR.II.B.R2	The difference between approved and non-approved navigation devices.
IR.II.B.R3	Common failure modes of flight and navigation instruments.
IR.II.B.R4	The limitations of electronic flight bags.
IR.II.B.R5	Failure to ensure currency of navigation databases.
Skills	The applicant demonstrates the ability to:
IR.II.B.S1	Operate and manage installed instruments and navigation equipment.

II. Preflight Procedures

Task	C. *Instrument Flight Deck Check*
References	14 CFR part 91; FAA-8083-2, FAA-H-8083-3, FAA-H-8083-15, FAA-H-8083-25; AC 91.21-1; POH/AFM
Objective	To determine the applicant exhibits satisfactory knowledge, risk management, and skills associated with conducting a preflight check on the airplane's instruments necessary for an IFR flight.
Knowledge	The applicant demonstrates understanding of:
IR.II.C.K1	Purpose of performing an instrument flight deck check and how to detect possible defects.
IR.II.C.K2	IFR airworthiness, to include airplane inspection requirements and required equipment for IFR flight.
IR.II.C.K3	Required procedures, documentation, and limitations of flying with inoperative equipment.
Risk Management	The applicant demonstrates the ability to identify, assess and mitigate risks, encompassing:
IR.II.C.R1	Operating with inoperative equipment.
IR.II.C.R2	Operating with outdated navigation publications or databases.
Skills	The applicant demonstrates the ability to:
IR.II.C.S1	Perform preflight inspection by following the checklist appropriate to the airplane and determine that the airplane is in a condition for safe instrument flight.

III. Air Traffic Control Clearances and Procedures

Task	A. Compliance with Air Traffic Control Clearances
References	14 CFR parts 61, 91; FAA-H-8083-15; AIM
Objective	To determine the applicant exhibits satisfactory knowledge, risk management, and skills associated with ATC clearances and procedures solely by reference to instruments. **Note:** See Appendix 7: Aircraft, Equipment, and Operational Requirements & Limitations for related considerations.
Knowledge	The applicant demonstrates understanding of:
IR.III.A.K1	Elements and procedures related to ATC clearances and pilot/controller responsibilities for departure, en route, and arrival phases of flight including clearance void times.
IR.III.A.K2	PIC emergency authority.
IR.III.A.K3	Lost communication procedures and procedures for flights outside of radar environments.
Risk Management	The applicant demonstrates the ability to identify, assess and mitigate risks, encompassing:
IR.III.A.R1	Failure to fully understand an ATC clearance.
IR.III.A.R2	Inappropriate, incomplete, or incorrect ATC clearances.
IR.III.A.R3	ATC clearance inconsistent with airplane performance and/or navigation capability.
IR.III.A.R4	ATC clearance intended for other aircraft with similar call signs.
Skills	The applicant demonstrates the ability to:
IR.III.A.S1	Correctly copy, read back, interpret, and comply with simulated and/or actual ATC clearances in a timely manner using standard phraseology as provided in the Aeronautical Information Manual.
IR.III.A.S2	Correctly set communication frequencies, navigation systems (identifying when appropriate), and transponder codes in compliance with the ATC clearance.
IR.III.A.S3	Use the current and appropriate paper or electronic navigation publications.
IR.III.A.S4	Intercept all courses, radials, and bearings appropriate to the procedure, route, or clearance in a timely manner.
IR.III.A.S5	Maintain the applicable airspeed ±10 knots, headings ±10°, altitude ±100 feet; and track a course, radial, or bearing within ¾-scale deflection of the CDI.
IR.III.A.S6	Demonstrate SRM.
IR.III.A.S7	Perform the appropriate airplane checklist items relative to the phase of flight.

III. Air Traffic Control Clearances and Procedures

Task	B. Holding Procedures
References	14 CFR parts 61, 91; FAA-H-8083-15, FAA-H-8083-16; AIM
Objective	To determine the applicant exhibits satisfactory knowledge, risk management, and skills associated with holding procedures solely by reference to instruments.
Knowledge	The applicant demonstrates understanding of:
IR.III.B.K1	Elements related to holding procedures, including reporting criteria, appropriate speeds, and recommended entry procedures for standard, published, and non-published holding patterns.
Risk Management	The applicant demonstrates the ability to identify, assess and mitigate risks, encompassing:
IR.III.B.R1	Recalculating fuel reserves if assigned an unanticipated expect further clearance (EFC) time.
IR.III.B.R2	Scenarios and circumstances that could result in minimum fuel or the need to declare an emergency.
IR.III.B.R3	Scenarios that could lead to holding, including deteriorating weather at the planned destination.
IR.III.B.R4	Improper holding entry and improper wind correction while holding.
Skills	The applicant demonstrates the ability to:
IR.III.B.S1	Explain and use an entry procedure that ensures the airplane remains within the holding pattern airspace for a standard, nonstandard, published, or non-published holding pattern.
IR.III.B.S2	Change to the holding airspeed appropriate for the altitude or airplane when 3 minutes or less from, but prior to arriving at, the holding fix and set appropriate power as needed for fuel conservation.
IR.III.B.S3	Recognize arrival at the holding fix and promptly initiate entry into the holding pattern.
IR.III.B.S4	Maintain airspeed ±10 knots, altitude ±100 feet, selected headings within ±10°, and track a selected course, radial, or bearing within ¾-scale deflection of the CDI.
IR.III.B.S5	Use proper wind correction procedures to maintain the desired pattern and to arrive over the fix as close as possible to a specified time and maintain pattern leg lengths when specified.
IR.III.B.S6	Use an MFD and other graphical navigation displays, if installed, to monitor position in relation to the desired flightpath during holding.
IR.III.B.S7	Comply with ATC reporting requirements and restrictions associated with the holding pattern.
IR.III.B.S8	Demonstrate SRM.

IV. Flight by Reference to Instruments

Task	A. Instrument Flight
References	14 CFR part 61; FAA-8083-2, FAA-H-8083-15
Objective	To determine the applicant exhibits satisfactory knowledge, risk management, and skills associated with performing basic instrument flight maneuvers solely by reference to instruments.
Knowledge	The applicant demonstrates understanding of:
IR.IV.A.K1	Elements related to attitude instrument flying during straight-and-level flight, climbs, turns, and descents while conducting various instrument flight procedures.
IR.IV.A.K2	Interpretation, operation, and limitations of pitch, bank, and power instruments.
IR.IV.A.K3	Normal and abnormal instrument indications and operations.
Risk Management	The applicant demonstrates the ability to identify, assess and mitigate risks, encompassing:
IR.IV.A.R1	Situations that can affect physiology and degrade instrument cross-check.
IR.IV.A.R2	Spatial disorientation and optical illusions.
IR.IV.A.R3	Flying unfamiliar airplanes, or operating with unfamiliar flight display systems and avionics.
Skills	The applicant demonstrates the ability to:
IR.IV.A.S1	Maintain altitude ±100 feet during level flight, selected headings ±10°, airspeed ±10 knots, and bank angles ±5° during turns.
IR.IV.A.S2	Use proper instrument cross-check and interpretation, and apply the appropriate pitch, bank, power, and trim corrections when applicable.

IV. Flight by Reference to Instruments

Task	B. Recovery from Unusual Flight Attitudes
References	14 CFR part 61; FAA-H-8083-15
Objective	To determine the applicant exhibits satisfactory knowledge, risk management, and skills associated with recovering from unusual flight attitudes solely by reference to instruments.
Knowledge	The applicant demonstrates understanding of:
IR.IV.B.K1	Procedures for recovery from unusual flight attitudes.
IR.IV.B.K2	Unusual flight attitude causal factors, including physiological factors, system and equipment failures, and environmental factors.
Risk Management	The applicant demonstrates the ability to identify, assess and mitigate risks, encompassing:
IR.IV.B.R1	Situations that could lead to loss of control or unusual flight attitudes (e.g., stress, task saturation, and distractions).
IR.IV.B.R2	Failure to recognize an unusual flight attitude and follow the proper recovery procedure.
Skills	The applicant demonstrates the ability to:
IR.IV.B.S1	Use proper instrument cross-check and interpretation to identify an unusual attitude (including both nose-high and nose-low), and apply the appropriate pitch, bank, and power corrections, in the correct sequence, to return to a stabilized level flight attitude.

V. Navigation Systems

Task	A. Intercepting and Tracking Navigational Systems and Arcs
References	14 CFR parts 61, 91; FAA-H-8083-15, FAA-H-8083-16; AFM; AIM *Note: The evaluator must reference the manufacturer's equipment supplement(s) as necessary for appropriate limitations, procedures, etc.*
Objective	To determine the applicant exhibits satisfactory knowledge, risk management, and skills associated with intercepting and tracking navigation aids and arcs solely by reference to instruments.
Knowledge	The applicant demonstrates understanding of:
IR.V.A.K1	Ground-based navigation (orientation, course determination, equipment, tests and regulations) including procedures for intercepting and tracking courses and arcs.
IR.V.A.K2	Satellite-based navigation (orientation, course determination, equipment, tests and regulations, interference, appropriate use of databases, Receiver Autonomous Integrity Monitoring (RAIM), and Wide Area Augmentation System (WAAS)) including procedures for intercepting and tracking courses and arcs.
Risk Management	The applicant demonstrates the ability to identify, assess and mitigate risks, encompassing:
IR.V.A.R1	Failure to manage automated navigation and autoflight systems.
IR.V.A.R2	Distractions, loss of situational awareness, and/or improper task management.
IR.V.A.R3	Limitations of the navigation system in use.
Skills	The applicant demonstrates the ability to:
IR.V.A.S1	Tune and correctly identify the navigation facility/program the navigation system and verify system accuracy as appropriate for the equipment installed in the airplane.
IR.V.A.S2	Determine airplane position relative to the navigational facility or waypoint.
IR.V.A.S3	Set and correctly orient to the course to be intercepted.
IR.V.A.S4	Intercept the specified course at appropriate angle, inbound to or outbound from a navigational facility or waypoint.
IR.V.A.S5	Maintain airspeed ±10 knots, altitude ±100 feet, and selected headings ±5°.
IR.V.A.S6	Apply proper correction to maintain a course, allowing no more than ¾-scale deflection of the CDI. If a DME arc is selected, maintain that arc ±1 nautical mile.
IR.V.A.S7	Recognize navigational system or facility failure, and when required, report the failure to ATC.
IR.V.A.S8	Use an MFD and other graphical navigation displays, if installed, to monitor position, track wind drift, and to maintain situational awareness.
IR.V.A.S9	Properly use the autopilot, if installed, to intercept courses.

V. Navigation Systems

Task	B. Departure, En Route, and Arrival Operations
References	14 CFR parts 61, 91; FAA-H-8083-15, FAA-H-8083-16; AC 91-74; AFM; AIM
Objective	To determine the applicant exhibits satisfactory knowledge, risk management, and skills associated with IFR departure, en route, and arrival operations solely by reference to instruments. **Note:** *See Appendix 7: Aircraft, Equipment, and Operational Requirements & Limitations for related considerations.*
Knowledge	The applicant demonstrates understanding of:
IR.V.B.K1	Elements related to ATC routes, including departure procedures (DPs) and associated climb gradients; arrival procedures (STARs) and associated constraints.
IR.V.B.K2	Pilot/controller responsibilities, communication procedures, and ATC services available to pilots.
Risk Management	The applicant demonstrates the ability to identify, assess and mitigate risks, encompassing:
IR.V.B.R1	Failure to communicate with ATC or follow published procedures.
IR.V.B.R2	Failure to recognize limitations of traffic avoidance equipment.
IR.V.B.R3	Failure to use see and avoid techniques when possible.
Skills	The applicant demonstrates the ability to:
IR.V.B.S1	Select, identify (as necessary) and use the appropriate communication and navigation facilities associated with the proposed flight.
IR.V.B.S2	Perform the appropriate airplane checklist items relative to the phase of flight.
IR.V.B.S3	Use the current and appropriate paper or electronic navigation publications..
IR.V.B.S4	Establish two-way communications with the proper controlling agency, use proper phraseology and comply, in a timely manner, with all ATC instructions and airspace restrictions as well as exhibit adequate knowledge of communication failure procedures.
IP.V.B.S5	Intercept all courses, radials, and bearings appropriate to the procedure, route, or clearance in a timely manner.
IR.V.B.S6	Comply with all applicable charted procedures.
IR.V.B.S7	Maintain airspeed ±10 knots, altitude ±100 feet, and selected headings ±10°, and apply proper correction to maintain a course allowing no more than ¾-scale deflection of the CDI.
IR V.B.S8	Update/interpret weather in flight.
IR.V.B.S9	Explain and use flight deck displays of digital weather and aeronautical information, as applicable.
IR.V.B.S10	Demonstrate SRM.

VI. Instrument Approach Procedures

Task	A. Nonprecision Approach
References	14 CFR parts 61, 91; FAA-H-8083-15, FAA-H-8083-16; IFP, AIM, AC 120-108
Objective	To determine the applicant exhibits satisfactory knowledge, risk management, and skills associated with performing nonprecision approach procedures solely by reference to instruments. **Note:** See Appendix 7: Aircraft, Equipment, and Operational Requirements & Limitations for related considerations.
Knowledge	The applicant demonstrates understanding of:
IR.VI.A.K1	Procedures and limitations associated with a nonprecision approach, including the differences between Localizer Performance (LP) and Lateral Navigation (LNAV) approach guidance.
IR.VI.A.K2	Navigation system annunciations expected during an RNAV approach.
Risk Management	The applicant demonstrates the ability to identify, assess and mitigate risks, encompassing:
IR.VI.A.R1	Descending below the minimum descent altitude (MDA) without proper visual references.
IR.VI.A.R2	Deteriorating weather conditions on approach.
IR.VI.A.R3	An unstable approach, including excessive descent rates.
IR.VI.A.R4	Failure to ensure proper airplane configuration during an approach and missed approach.
IR.VI.A.R5	Failure to manage automated navigation and autoflight systems.
Skills	The applicant demonstrates the ability to:
IR.VI.A.S1	Accomplish the nonprecision instrument approaches selected by the evaluator.
IR.VI.A.S2	Establish two-way communications with ATC appropriate for the phase of flight or approach segment, and use proper communication phraseology.
IR.VI.A.S3	Select, tune, identify, and confirm the operational status of navigation equipment to be used for the approach.
IR.VI.A.S4	Comply with all clearances issued by ATC or the evaluator.
IR.VI.A.S5	Recognize if any flight instrumentation is inaccurate or inoperative, and take appropriate action.
IR.VI.A.S6	Advise ATC or the evaluator if unable to comply with a clearance.
IR.VI.A.S7	Establish the appropriate airplane configuration and airspeed considering turbulence and windshear, and complete the airplane checklist items appropriate to the phase of the flight.
IR.VI.A.S8	Maintain altitude ±100 feet, selected heading ±10°, airspeed ±10 knots, prior to beginning the final approach segment.
IR.VI.A.S9	Apply adjustments to the published MDA and visibility criteria for the aircraft approach category, as appropriate, for factors that include NOTAMs, inoperative airplane or navigation equipment, or inoperative visual aids associated with the landing environment, etc.
IR.VI.A.S10	Establish a stabilized descent to the appropriate altitude.
IR.VI.A.S11	For the final approach segment, maintain no more than a ¾-scale deflection of the CDI, maintain airspeed ±10 knots, and altitude, if applicable, above MDA, +100/-0 feet, to the Visual Descent Point (VDP) or Missed Approach Point (MAP).
IR.VI.A.S12	Execute the missed approach procedure if the required visual references for the intended runway are not distinctly visible and identifiable at the appropriate point or altitude for the approach profile.
IR.VI.A.S13	Execute a normal landing from a straight-in or circling approach when instructed by the evaluator.
IR.VI.A.S14	Use an MFD and other graphical navigation displays, if installed, to monitor position, track wind drift, and to maintain situational awareness.

VI. Instrument Approach Procedures

Task	B. Precision Approach
References	14 CFR parts 61, 91; FAA-H-8083-15, FAA-H-8083-16; IFP; AIM
Objective	To determine the applicant exhibits satisfactory knowledge, risk management, and skills associated with performing precision approach procedures solely by reference to instruments. **Note:** See Appendix 7: Aircraft, Equipment, and Operational Requirements & Limitations for related considerations.
Knowledge	The applicant demonstrates understanding of:
IR.VI.B.K1	Procedures and limitations associated with a precision approach, including determining required descent rates and adjusting minimums in the case of inoperative equipment.
Risk Management	The applicant demonstrates the ability to identify, assess and mitigate risks, encompassing:
IR.VI.B.R1	Failure to immediately initiate the missed approach at Decision Altitude (DA)/Decision Height (DH) if the required visual references are not visible.
IR.VI.B.R2	Deteriorating weather conditions on approach.
IR.VI.B.R3	An unstable approach including excessive descent rates.
IR.VI.B.R4	Failure to ensure proper airplane configuration during an approach and missed approach.
IR.VI.B.R5	Failure to manage automated navigation and autoflight systems.
Skills	The applicant demonstrates the ability to:
IR.VI.B.S1	Accomplish the precision instrument approach(es) selected by the evaluator.
IR.VI.B.S2	Establish two-way communications with ATC appropriate for the phase of flight or approach segment, and use proper communication phraseology.
IR.VI.B.S3	Select, tune, identify, and confirm the operational status of navigation equipment to be used for the approach.
IR.VI.B.S4	Comply with all clearances issued by ATC or the evaluator.
IR.VI.B.S5	Recognize if any flight instrumentation is inaccurate or inoperative, and take appropriate action.
IR.VI.B.S6	Advise ATC or the evaluator if unable to comply with a clearance.
IR.VI.B.S7	Establish the appropriate airplane configuration and airspeed considering turbulence and windshear, and complete the airplane checklist items appropriate to the phase of the flight.
IR.VI.B.S8	Maintain altitude ±100 feet, selected heading ±10°, airspeed ±10 knots, prior to beginning the final approach segment.
IR VI.B.S9	Apply adjustments to the published DA/DH and visibility criteria for the aircraft approach category, as appropriate, for factors that include NOTAMs, Inoperative airplane or navigation equipment, or inoperative visual aids associated with the landing environment, etc. .
IR.VI.B.S10	Establish a predetermined rate of descent at the point where vertical guidance begins, which approximates that required for the airplane to follow the vertical guidance.
IR.VI.B.S11	Maintain a stabilized final approach from the Final Approach Fix (FAF) to DA/DH allowing no more than ¾-scale deflection of either the vertical or lateral guidance indications and maintain the desired airspeed ±10 knots.
IR.VI.B.S12	Immediately initiate the missed approach procedure when at the DA/DH, and the required visual references for the runway are not unmistakably visible and identifiable.
IR.VI.B.S13	Transition to a normal landing approach (missed approach for seaplanes) only when the airplane is in a position from which a descent to a landing on the runway can be made at a normal rate of descent using normal maneuvering.
IR.VI.B.S14	Maintain a stabilized visual flight path from the DA/DH to the runway aiming point where a normal landing may be accomplished within the touchdown zone.
IR.VI.B.S15	Use an MFD and other graphical navigation displays, if installed, to monitor position, track wind drift, and to maintain situational awareness.

VI. Instrument Approach Procedures

Task	C. Missed Approach
References	14 CFR parts 61, 91; FAA-H-8083-15; IFP; AIM
Objective	To determine the applicant exhibits satisfactory knowledge, risk management, and skills associated with performing a missed approach procedure solely by reference to instruments.
Knowledge	The applicant demonstrates understanding of:
IR.VI.C.K1	Elements related to missed approach procedures and limitations associated with standard instrument approaches, including while using a FMS and/or autopilot, if equipped.
Risk Management	The applicant demonstrates the ability to identify, assess and mitigate risks, encompassing:
IR.VI.C.R1	Failure to follow prescribed procedures.
IR.VI.C.R2	Holding, diverting, or electing to fly the approach again.
IR.VI.C.R3	Failure to ensure proper airplane configuration during an approach and missed approach.
IR.VI.C.R4	Factors that might lead to executing a missed approach procedure before the missed approach point or to a go-around below DA/MDA.
IR.VI.C.R5	Failure to manage automated navigation and autoflight systems.
Skills	The applicant demonstrates the ability to:
IR.VI.C.S1	Initiate the missed approach promptly by applying power, establishing a climb attitude, and configuring the airplane in accordance with the airplane's manufacturer's recommendations.
IR.VI.C.S2	Report to ATC upon beginning the missed approach procedure.
IR.VI.C.S3	Comply with the published or alternate missed approach procedure.
IR.VI.C.S4	Advise ATC or the evaluator if unable to comply with a clearance, restriction, or climb gradient.
IR.VI.C.S5	Follow the recommended checklist items appropriate to the missed approach/go-around procedure.
IR.VI.C.S6	Request, if appropriate, ATC clearance to the alternate airport, clearance limit, or as directed by the evaluator.
IR.VI.C.S7	Maintain the recommended airspeed ±10 knots; heading, course, or bearing ±10°; and altitude(s) ±100 feet during the missed approach procedure.
IR.VI.C.S8	Use an MFD and other graphical navigation displays, if installed, to monitor position and track to help navigate the missed approach.
IR.VI.C.S9	Demonstrate SRM.

VI. Instrument Approach Procedures

Task	D. Circling Approach
References	14 CFR parts 61, 91; FAA-H-8083-15; IFP; AIM
Objective	To determine the applicant exhibits satisfactory knowledge, risk management, and skills associated with performing a circling approach procedure.
Knowledge	The applicant demonstrates understanding of:
IR.VI.D.K1	Elements related to circling approach procedures and limitations including approach categories and related airspeed restrictions.
Risk Management	The applicant demonstrates the ability to identify, assess and mitigate risks, encompassing:
IR.VI.D.R1	Failure to follow prescribed circling approach procedures.
IR.VI.D.R2	Executing a circling approach at night or with marginal visibility.
IR.VI.D.R3	Losing visual contact with an identifiable part of the airport.
IR.VI.D.R4	Failure to manage automated navigation and autoflight systems.
IR.VI.D.R5	Failure to maintain an appropriate airspeed while circling.
IR.VI.D.R6	Low altitude maneuvering including stall, spin, or CFIT.
IR.VI.D.R7	Executing an improper missed approach after the MAP while circling.
Skills	The applicant demonstrates the ability to:
IR.VI.D.S1	Select and comply with the circling approach procedure considering turbulence, windshear, and the maneuvering capabilities of the airplane.
IR.VI.D.S2	Confirm the direction of traffic and adhere to all restrictions and instructions issued by ATC or the evaluator.
IR.VI.D.S3	Maneuver the airplane, at or above the MDA, 90° or more from the final approach course, on a flightpath permitting a normal landing on a suitable runway.
IR.VI.D.S4	Avoid circling beyond visibility requirements and maintain the appropriate circling altitude until in a position from which a descent to a normal landing can be made.
IR.VI.D.S5	Establish the approach and landing configuration for the situation and maintain altitude +100/-0 feet until a descent to a normal landing can be made.
IR.VI.D.S6	Demonstrate SRM.

VI. Instrument Approach Procedures

Task	E. Landing from an Instrument Approach
References	14 CFR parts 61, 91; FAA-H-8083-15; AIM
Objective	To determine the applicant exhibits satisfactory knowledge, risk management, and skills associated with performing the procedures for a landing from an instrument approach.
Knowledge	The applicant demonstrates understanding of:
IR.VI.E.K1	Elements related to the pilot's responsibilities, and the environmental, operational, and meteorological factors that affect landing from a straight-in or circling approach.
IR.VI.E.K2	Airport signs, markings and lighting, to include approach lighting systems.
Risk Management	The applicant demonstrates the ability to identify, assess and mitigate risks, encompassing:
IR.VI.E.R1	Attempting to land from an unstable approach.
IR.VI.E.R2	Flying below the glidepath.
IR.VI.E.R3	Transitioning from instrument to visual references for landing.
Skills	The applicant demonstrates the ability to:
IR.VI.E.S1	Transition at the DA/DH, MDA, or visual descent point VDP to a visual flight condition, allowing for safe visual maneuvering and a normal landing.
IR.VI.E.S2	Adhere to all ATC or evaluator advisories, such as NOTAMs, windshear, wake turbulence, runway surface, braking conditions, and other operational considerations.
IR.VI.E.S3	Complete the appropriate checklist.
IR.VI.E.S4	Maintain positive airplane control throughout the landing maneuver.
IR.VI.E.S5	Demonstrate SRM.

VII. Emergency Operations

Task	A. Loss of Communications
References	14 CFR parts 61, 91; AIM
Objective	To determine the applicant exhibits satisfactory knowledge, risk management, and skills associated with loss of communications while operating solely by reference to instruments.
Knowledge	The applicant demonstrates understanding of:
IR.VII.A.K1	Procedures to follow in the event of lost communication during various phases of flight, including techniques for reestablishing communications, when it is acceptable to deviate from an IFR clearance, and when to begin an approach at the destination.
Risk Management	The applicant demonstrates the ability to identify, assess and mitigate risks, encompassing:
IR.VII.A.R1	Possible reasons for loss of communication.
IR.VII.A.R2	Failure to follow procedures for lost communications.
Skills	The applicant demonstrates the ability to:
IR.VII.A.S1	Recognize a simulated loss of communication.
IR.VII.A.S2	Simulate actions to re-establish communication.
IR.VII.A.S3	Determine whether to continue to flight plan destination or deviate.
IR.VII.A.S4	Determine appropriate time to begin an approach.

VII. Emergency Operations

Task	B. One Engine Inoperative (Simulated) during Straight-and-Level Flight and Turns (AMEL, AMES)
References	14 CFR 61; FAA-H-8083-3, FAA-H-8083-15
Objective	To determine the applicant exhibits satisfactory knowledge, risk management and skills associated with flight solely by reference to instruments with one engine inoperative.
Knowledge	The applicant demonstrates understanding of:
IR.VII.B.K1	Procedures used if engine failure occurs during straight-and-level flight and turns while on instruments.
Risk Management	The applicant demonstrates the ability to identify, assess and mitigate risks, encompassing:
IR.VII.B.R1	Failure to identify the inoperative engine correctly.
IR.VII.B.R2	Inability to climb or maintain altitude with an inoperative engine.
IR.VII.B.R3	Low altitude maneuvering including stall, spin, or CFIT.
IR.VII.B.R4	Distractions, loss of situational awareness, and/or improper task management.
IR.VII.B.R5	Fuel management during single-engine operation.
Skills	The applicant demonstrates the ability to:
IR.VII.B.S1	Promptly recognize an engine failure and maintain positive airplane control.
IR.VII.B.S2	Set the engine controls, reduce drag, identify and verify the inoperative engine, and simulate feathering of the propeller on the inoperative engine. (Evaluator should then establish zero thrust on the inoperative engine).
IR.VII.B.S3	Establish the best engine-inoperative airspeed and trim the airplane.
IR.VII.B.S4	Use flight controls in the proper combination as recommended by the manufacturer, or as required to maintain best performance, and trim as required.
IR.VII.B.S5	Verify the prescribed checklist procedures normally used for securing the inoperative engine.
IR.VII.B.S6	Attempt to determine and resolve the reason for the engine failure.
IR.VII.B.S7	Monitor all engine control functions and make necessary adjustments.
IR.VII.B.S8	Maintain the specified altitude ±100 feet or minimum sink rate if applicable, airspeed ±10 knots, and the specified heading ±10°.
IR.VII.B.S9	Assess the airplane's performance capability and decide an appropriate action to ensure a safe landing.
IR.VII.B.S10	Avoid loss of airplane control, or attempted flight contrary to the operating limitations of the airplane.
IR.VII.B.S11	Demonstrate SRM.

VII. Emergency Operations

Task	**C. Instrument Approach and Landing with an Inoperative Engine (Simulated) (AMEL, AMES)** **Note:** See Appendix 7: Aircraft, Equipment, and Operational Requirements & Limitations for related considerations.
References	14 CFR parts 61, 91; FAA-H-8083-3, FAA-H-8083-15, IFP
Objective	To determine that the applicant exhibits satisfactory knowledge, risk management, and skills associated with executing a published instrument approach solely by reference to instruments with one engine inoperative.
Knowledge	The applicant demonstrates understanding of:
IR.VII.C.K1	Instrument approach procedures with one engine inoperative.
Risk Management	The applicant demonstrates the ability to identify, assess, and mitigate risks, encompassing:
IR.VII.C.R1	Failure to plan for engine failure during approach and landing.
IR.VII.C.R2	Distractions, loss of situational awareness, and/or improper task management.
IR.VII.C.R3	Single-engine performance.
Skills	The applicant demonstrates the ability to:
IR.VII.C.S1	Promptly recognize a engine failure and maintain positive airplane control. Set the engine controls, reduce drag, identify and verify the inoperative engine, and simulate feathering of the propeller on the inoperative engine. (Evaluator should then establish zero thrust on the inoperative engine).
IR.VII.C.S2	Use flight controls in the proper combination as recommended by the manufacturer, or as required to maintain best performance, and trim as required.
IR.VII.C.S3	Follow the manufacturer's recommended emergency procedures.
IR.VII.C.S4	Monitor the operating engine and make necessary adjustments.
IR.VII.C.S5	Request and follow an actual or a simulated ATC clearance for an instrument approach.
IR.VII.C.S6	Maintain altitude ±100 feet or minimum sink rate if applicable, airspeed ±10 knots, and selected heading ±10°.
IR.VII.C.S7	Establish a rate of descent that will ensure arrival at the MDA or DH/DA with the airplane in a position from which a descent to a landing on the intended runway can be made, either straight in or circling as appropriate.
IR.VII.C.S8	On final approach segment, maintain vertical (as applicable) and lateral guidance within ¾-scale deflection.
IR.VII.C.S9	Avoid loss of airplane control, or attempted flight contrary to the operating limitations of the airplane.
IR.VII.C.S10	Comply with the published criteria for the aircraft approach category if circling.
IR.VII.C.S11	Execute a normal landing.
IR.VII.C.S12	Complete the appropriate checklist.

VII. Emergency Operations

Task	D. *Approach with Loss of Primary Flight Instrument Indicators*
References	14 CFR parts 61, 91; FAA-H-8083-15; IFP
Objective	To determine the applicant exhibits satisfactory knowledge, risk management, and skills associated with performing an approach solely by reference to instruments with the loss of primary flight control instruments.
Knowledge	The applicant demonstrates understanding of:
IR.VII.D.K1	Recognizing if primary flight instruments are inaccurate or inoperative, and advising ATC or the evaluator.
IR.VII.D.K2	Common failure modes of vacuum and electric attitude instruments and how to correct or minimize the effect of their loss.
Risk Management	The applicant demonstrates the ability to identify, assess and mitigate risks, encompassing:
IR.VII.D.R1	Use of secondary flight displays when primary displays have failed.
IR.VII.D.R2	Failure to maintain airplane control.
IR.VII.D.R3	Distractions, loss of situational awareness, and/or improper task management.
Skills	The applicant demonstrates the ability to:
IR.VII.D.S1	Advise ATC or the evaluator of if unable to comply with a clearance.
IR.VII.D.S2	Complete a nonprecision instrument approach without the use of the primary flight instruments using the skill elements of the nonprecision approach Task (See Area of Operation VI, Task A).
IR.VII.D.S3	Demonstrate SRM.

VIII. Postflight Procedures

Task	A. *Checking Instruments and Equipment*
References	14 CFR parts 61, 91
Objective	To determine the applicant exhibits satisfactory knowledge, risk management, and skills associated with checking flight instruments and equipment during postflight.
Knowledge	The applicant demonstrates understanding of:
IR.VIII.A.K1	Procedures for checking the functionality of all installed instruments and navigation equipment.
Risk Management	The applicant demonstrates the ability to identify, assess and mitigate risks, encompassing:
IR.VIII.A.R1	Failure to perform a proper postflight inspection and properly document airplane discrepancies.
Skills	The applicant demonstrates the ability to:
IR.VIII.A.S1	Conduct a postflight inspection, and document discrepancies and servicing requirements, if any.

Appendix Table of Contents

Appendix 1: The Knowledge Test Eligibility, Prerequisites, and Testing Centers

Knowledge Test Description

The knowledge test is an important part of the airman certification process. Applicants must pass the knowledge test before taking the practical test.

The knowledge test consists of objective, multiple-choice questions. There is a single correct response for each test question. Each test question is independent of other questions. A correct response to one question does not depend upon, or influence, the correct response to another.

Knowledge Test Tables

Test Code	Test Name	Number of Questions	Age	Allotted Time	Passing Score
AIF	Flight Instructor Instrument Airplane **(Added Rating)***	20	16	1.0	70
FIH	Flight Instructor Instrument Helicopter	50	16	2.5	70
FII	Flight Instructor Instrument Airplane	50	16	2.5	70
HIF	Flight Instructor Instrument Helicopter **(Added Rating)***	20	16	1.0	70
ICH	Instrument Rating Helicopter *Canadian Conversion*	40	15	2.0	70
ICP	Instrument Rating Airplane *Canadian Conversion*	40	15	2.0	70
IFP	Instrument Rating Foreign Pilot	50	n/a	2.5	70
IGI	Ground Instructor Instrument	50	16	2.5	70
IRA	Instrument Rating Airplane	60	15	2.5	70
IRH	Instrument Rating Helicopter	60	15	2.5	70

*See Rating Table in Appendix 4: The Practical Test – Eligibility and Prerequisites.

Knowledge Test Blueprint

IRA Knowledge Areas Required by 14 CFR part 61, section 61.65 to be on the Knowledge Test	Percent of Questions Per Test
Regulations	5 - 15%
IFR En Route and Approach Procedures	5 - 15%
Air Traffic Control and Procedures	5 - 20%
IFR Navigation	5 - 20%
Weather Reports, Critical Weather, Windshear and Forecasts	10 - 20%
Safe and Efficient IFR Operations	5 - 10%
Aeronautical Decision-Making	5 - 10%
Crew Resource Management (CRM)	5 - 10%
Total Number of Questions	60

English Language Standard

In accordance with the requirements of 14 CFR part 61, section 61.65(a)(2) the applicant must demonstrate the ability to read, write, speak, and understand the English language throughout the application and testing process. English language proficiency is required to communicate effectively with Air Traffic Control (ATC), to comply with ATC instructions, and to ensure clear and effective crew communication and coordination. Normal restatement of questions as would be done for a native English speaker is permitted, and does not constitute grounds for disqualification. The FAA Aviation English Language Standard (AELS) is the FAA evaluator's benchmark. It requires the applicant to demonstrate at least the International Civil Aviation Organization (ICAO) level 4 standard.

Knowledge Test Requirements

In order to take the IRA Knowledge Test, you must provide proper identification. To verify your eligibility to take the test, you must also provide one of the following in accordance with the requirements of 14 CFR part 61:

- 14 CFR part 61, section 61.35 lists the prerequisites for taking the knowledge test, to include the minimum age an applicant must be to take the test.
  - Received an endorsement, if required by this part, from an authorized instructor certifying that the applicant accomplished the appropriate ground-training or a home-study course required by this part for the certificate or rating sought and is prepared for the knowledge test;
  - Proper identification at the time of application that contains the applicant's—
    - o (i) Photograph;
    - o (ii) Signature;
    - o (iii) Date of birth; and
    - o (iv) If the permanent mailing address is a post office box number, then the applicant must provide a government-issued residential address.

- 14 CFR part 61, section 61.49 acceptable forms of retest authorization for **all** Instrument Rating tests:
  - An applicant retesting **after failure** is required to submit the applicable Airman Knowledge Test Report indicating failure, along with an endorsement from an authorized instructor who gave the applicant the required additional training. The endorsement must certify that the applicant is competent to pass the test. The test proctor must retain the original failed Airman Knowledge Test Report presented as authorization and attach it to the applicable sign-in/out log.

    Note: *If the applicant no longer possesses the original Airman Knowledge Test Report, he or she may request a duplicate replacement issued by the Airmen Certification Branch, https://www.faa.gov/licenses_certificates/ airmen_certification/test_results_replacement/.*

- Acceptable forms of authorization for Instrument Rating Airplane Canadian Conversion (ICP) only:
  - o Confirmation of Verification Letter issued by the Office of Foundational Business, Civil Aviation Division, Airmen Certification Branch (Knowledge Testing Authorization Requirements Matrix). https://www.faa.gov/training_testing/testing/media/testing_matrix.pdf
  - o Requires **no** instructor endorsement or other form of written authorization.

Knowledge Test Centers

The FAA authorizes hundreds of knowledge testing center locations that offer a full range of airman knowledge tests. For information on authorized testing centers and to register for the knowledge test, contact one of the providers listed at www.faa.gov.

Knowledge Test Registration

When you contact a knowledge testing center to register for a test, please be prepared to select a test date, choose a testing center, and make financial arrangements for test payment when you call. You may register for test(s) several weeks in advance, and you may cancel in accordance with the testing center's cancellation policy.

Appendix 2: Knowledge Test Procedures and Tips

Before starting the actual test, the testing center will provide an opportunity to practice navigating through the test. This practice or tutorial session may include sample questions to familiarize the applicant with the look and feel of the software. (e.g., selecting an answer, marking a question for later review, monitoring time remaining for the test, and other features of the testing software.)

Acceptable Materials

The applicant may use the following aids, reference materials, and test materials, as long as the material does not include actual test questions or answers:

Acceptable Materials	Unacceptable Materials	Notes
Supplement book provided by proctor	Written materials that are handwritten, printed, or electronic	Testing centers may provide calculators and/or deny the use of personal calculators.
All models of aviation-oriented calculators or small electronic calculators that perform only arithmetic functions	Electronic calculators incorporating permanent or continuous type memory circuits without erasure capability.	Unit Member (proctor) may prohibit the use of your calculator if he or she is unable to determine the calculator's erasure capability
Calculators with simple programmable memories, which allow addition to, subtraction from, or retrieval of one number from the memory; or simple functions, such as square root and percentages	Magnetic Cards, magnetic tapes, modules, computer chips, or any other device upon which pre-written programs or information related to the test can be stored and retrieved	Printouts of data must be surrendered at the completion of the test if the calculator incorporates this design feature.
Scales, straightedges, protractors, plotters, navigation computers, blank log sheets, holding pattern entry aids, and electronic or mechanical calculators that are directly related to the test	Dictionaries	Before, and upon completion of the test, while in the presence of the Unit Member, actuate the ON/OFF switch or RESET button, and perform any other function that ensures erasure of any data stored in memory circuits
Manufacturer's permanently inscribed instructions on the front and back of such aids, e.g., formulas, conversions, regulations, signals, weather data, holding pattern diagrams, frequencies, weight and balance formulas, and air traffic control procedures	Any booklet or manual containing instructions related to use of test aids	Unit Member makes the final determination regarding aids, reference materials, and test materials

Test Tips

When taking a knowledge test, please keep the following points in mind:

- Carefully read the instructions provided with the test.
- Answer each question in accordance with the latest regulations and guidance publications.
- Read each question carefully before looking at the answer options. You should clearly understand the problem before trying to solve it.
- After formulating a response, determine which answer option corresponds with your answer. The answer you choose should completely solve the problem.
- Remember that only one answer is complete and correct. The other possible answers are either incomplete or erroneous.

- If a certain question is difficult for you, mark it for review and return to it after you have answered the less difficult questions. This procedure will enable you to use the available time to maximum advantage.
- When solving a calculation problem, be sure to read all the associated notes.
- For questions involving use of a graph, you may request a printed copy that you can mark in computing your answer. This copy and all other notes and paperwork must be given to the testing center upon completion of the test.

Cheating or Other Unauthorized Conduct

To avoid test compromise, computer testing centers must follow strict security procedures established by the FAA and described in FAA Order 8080.6 (as amended), Conduct of Airman Knowledge Tests. The FAA has directed testing centers to terminate a test at any time a test unit member suspects that a cheating incident has occurred.

The FAA will investigate and, if the agency determines that cheating or unauthorized conduct has occurred, any airman certificate or rating you hold may be revoked. You will also be prohibited from applying for or taking any test for a certificate or rating under 14 CFR part 61 for a period of 1 year.

Testing Procedures for Applicants Requesting Special Accommodations

An applicant with learning or reading disability may request approval from the Airman Testing Branch through the local Flight Standards District Office (FSDO) or International Field Office/International Field Unit (IFO/IFU) to take airman knowledge test using one of the three options listed below, in preferential order:

Option 1: Use current testing facilities and procedures whenever possible.

Option 2: Use a self-contained, electronic device which pronounces and displays typed-in words (e.g., the Franklin Speaking Wordmaster®) to facilitate the testing process.

> **Note:** The device should consist of an electronic thesaurus that audibly pronounces typed-in words and presents them on a display screen. The device should also have a built-in headphone jack in order to avoid disturbing others during testing.

Option 3: Request the proctor's assistance in reading specific words or terms from the test questions and/or supplement book. To prevent compromising the testing process, the proctor must be an individual with no aviation background or expertise. The proctor may provide reading assistance only (i.e., no explanation of words or terms). When an applicant requests this option, the FSDO or IFO/IFU inspector must contact the Airman Testing Branch for assistance in selecting the test site and assisting the proctor. Before approving any option, the FSDO or IFO/IFU inspector must advise the applicant of the regulatory certification requirement to be able to read, write, speak, and understand the English language.

Appendix 3: Airman Knowledge Test Report

Immediately upon completion of the knowledge test, the applicant receives a printed Airman Knowledge Test Report (AKTR) documenting the score with the testing center's raised, embossed seal. The applicant must retain the original AKTR. The instructor must provide instruction in each area of deficiency and provide a logbook endorsement certifying that the applicant has demonstrated satisfactory knowledge in each area. When taking the practical test, the applicant must present the original AKTR to the evaluator, who is required to assess the noted areas of deficiency during the oral portion of the practical test.

An AKTR expires 24 calendar months after the month the applicant completes the knowledge test. If the AKTR expires before completion of the practical test, the applicant must retake the knowledge test.

To obtain a duplicate AKTR due to loss or destruction of the original, the applicant can send a signed request accompanied by a check or money order for $12.00, payable to the FAA to the following address:

Federal Aviation Administration
Airmen Certification Branch
P.O. Box 25082
Oklahoma City, OK 73125

To obtain a copy of the application form or a list of the information required, please see the Airmen Certification Branch webpage, https://www.faa.gov/licenses_certificates/airmen_certification/test_results_replacement/.

FAA Knowledge Test Question Coding

Each Task in the ACS includes an ACS code. This ACS code will ultimately be displayed on the AKTR to indicate what Task element was proven deficient on the knowledge test. Instructors can then provide remedial training in the deficient areas, and evaluators can re-test this element during the practical test.

The ACS coding consists of four elements. For example, this code is interpreted as follows:

IR.I.C.K4:

>**IR** = Applicable ACS (Instrument Rating – Airplane)
>**I** = Area of Operation (Preflight Preparation)
>**C** = Task (Cross-Country Flight Planning)
>**K4** = Task Element Knowledge 4 (Elements of an IFR flight plan.)

Knowledge test questions are linked to the ACS codes, which will ultimately replace the system of Learning Statement Codes (LSC). After this transition occurs, the AKTR will list an ACS code that correlates to a specific Task element for a given Area of Operation and Task. Remedial instruction and re-testing will be specific, targeted, and based on specified learning criteria. Similarly, a Notice of Disapproval for the practical test will use the ACS codes to identify the deficient Task elements.

The current knowledge test management system does not have the capability to print ACS codes. Until a new test management system is in place, the LSC (e.g., "PLT058") code will continue to be displayed on the AKTR. The LSC codes are linked to references leading to broad subject areas. By contrast, each ACS code is tied to a unique Task element in the ACS itself. Because of this fundamental difference, there is no one-to-one correlation between LSC codes and ACS codes.

Because all active knowledge test questions for the Instrument Rating Airplane (IRA) knowledge test have been aligned with the corresponding ACS, evaluators can continue to use LSC codes in conjunction with the ACS for the time being. The evaluator should look up the LSC code(s) on the applicant's AKTR in the Learning Statement Reference Guide available in the Learning Statement Reference Guide, https://www.faa.gov/training_testing/testing/media/LearningStatementReferenceGuide.pdf. After noting the subject area(s), the evaluator can use the corresponding Area(s) of Operation/Task(s) in the ACS to narrow the scope of material for retesting, and to evaluate the applicant's understanding of that material in the context of the appropriate ACS Area(s) of Operation and Task(s).

The Applicant Name Considerations for the Airman Knowledge Test Report (AKTR) and the Practical Test Application Form

The applicant uses his or her full legal name on the Airman Certificate and/or Rating Application, FAA Form 8710-1, using up to 50 characters (including spaces). The applicant may exclude some middle names as necessary to meet the 50-character limit. The AKTR may not reflect the applicant's full legal name and may differ slightly from the name presented for the practical test.

If the 8710-1 shows a middle name, the AKTR may show that middle name, the correct middle initial, or no entry. The application will process correctly using the Integrated Airman Certificate and Rating Application (IACRA) system, and the Airmen Certification Branch will accept it. If an incorrect middle initial, spelling variant or different middle name is on the AKTR, or if the AKTR has a first name variation of any kind, the evaluator must attach an explanation and a scan or copy of the applicant's photo identification and attach it to the IACRA or paper application. If the last name on the AKTR has a different spelling or suffix, an IACRA application is not possible. The applicant must use a paper application, and the evaluator must include an explanation and copy of the applicant's photo identification to avoid a correction notice.

Appendix 4: The Practical Test – Eligibility and Prerequisites

The prerequisite requirements and general eligibility for a practical test and the specific requirements for the original issuance of an instrument rating in the airplane can be found in 14 CFR part 61, sections 61.39 and 61.65.

If an applicant holds both single-engine and multiengine class ratings on a pilot certificate and takes the instrument rating practical test in a single-engine airplane, the certificate issued must bear the limitation "Multiengine Limited to VFR Only." If the applicant takes the test in a multiengine airplane, the instrument privileges will be automatically conferred for the airplane single-engine rating.

Additional Instrument Rating Desired

If you hold an instrument rating in another category and adding Instrument – Airplane, you are required to complete the Task(s) indicated in the following table:

Area of Operation	Required Task(s)
I	None
II	A,C
III	None
IV	All
V	None
VI	All
VII	All [1]
VIII	All

Removal of the "Airplane Multiengine VFR Only" Limitation

The removal of the "Airplane Multiengine VFR Only" limitation, at the private pilot or commercial pilot certificate level, requires an applicant to satisfactorily perform the following Area of Operation and Tasks from the Instrument Rating– Airplane ACS in a multiengine airplane that has a manufacturer's published V_{MC} speed.

VII. Emergency Operations

Task B: One Engine Inoperative during Straight-and-Level Flight and Turns (AMEL, AMES)

Task C: Instrument Approach and Landing with an Inoperative Engine (Simulated) (AMEL, AMES)

---

[1] Tasks B and C are applicable *only* to *multiengine airplanes.*

Appendix 5: Practical Test Roles, Responsibilities, and Outcomes

Applicant Responsibilities

The applicant is responsible for mastering the established standards for knowledge, risk management, and skill elements in all Tasks appropriate to the certificate and rating sought. The applicant should use this ACS, its references, and the Applicant's Practical Test Checklist in this Appendix in preparation to take the practical test.

Instructor Responsibilities

The instructor is responsible for training the applicant to meet the established standards for knowledge, risk management, and skill elements in all Tasks appropriate to the certificate and rating sought. The instructor should use this ACS and its references as part of preparing the applicant to take the practical test and, if necessary, in retraining the applicant to proficiency in all subject(s) missed on the knowledge test.

Evaluator Responsibilities

An evaluator is:

- Aviation Safety Inspector (ASI);
- Pilot examiner (other than administrative pilot examiners);
- Training center evaluator (TCE);
- Chief instructor, assistant chief instructor or check instructor of pilot school holding examining authority; or
- Instrument Flight Instructor (CFII) conducting an instrument proficiency check (IPC).

The evaluator who conducts the practical test is responsible for determining that the applicant meets the established standards of aeronautical knowledge, risk management, and skills (flight proficiency) for the Tasks in the appropriate ACS. This responsibility also includes verifying the experience requirements specified for a certificate or rating.

Prior to beginning the practical test, the evaluator must also determine that the applicant meets FAA Aviation English Language Proficiency Standards by verifying that he or she can understand ATC instructions and communicate in English at a level that is understandable to ATC and other pilots. The evaluator should use the procedures outlined in the AC 60-28, English Language Skill Standard required by 14 CFR parts 61, 63, 65, and 107, as amended, when evaluating the applicant's ability to meet the standard.

The evaluator must develop a Plan of Action (POA), written in English, to conduct the practical test. It must include all of the required Areas of Operation and Tasks. The POA must include a scenario that evaluates as many of the required Areas of Operation and Tasks as possible. As the scenario unfolds during the test, the evaluator will introduce problems and emergencies that the applicant must manage. The evaluator has the discretion to modify the POA in order to accommodate unexpected situations as they arise. For example, the evaluator may elect to suspend and later resume a scenario in order to assess certain Tasks.

In the integrated ACS framework, the Areas of Operation contain Tasks that include "Knowledge" elements (such as K1), "risk management" elements (such as R1), and "skill" elements (such as S1). Knowledge and risk management elements are primarily evaluated during the knowledge testing phase of the airman certification process. The evaluator must assess the applicant on all skill elements for each Task included in each Area of Operation of the ACS, unless otherwise noted. The evaluator administering the practical test has the discretion to combine Tasks/elements as appropriate to testing scenarios.

The required minimum elements to include in the POA, unless otherwise noted, from each applicable Task are as follows:

- at least one knowledge element;
- at least one risk management element;
- all skill elements; and
- any Task elements in which the applicant was shown to be deficient on the knowledge test.

Note: *Task elements added to the POA on the basis of being listed on the AKTR may satisfy the other minimum Task element requirements. The missed items on the AKTR are not required to be added in addition to the minimum Task element requirements.*

There is no expectation for testing every knowledge element and risk management element in a Task, but the evaluator has discretion to sample as needed to ensure the applicant's mastery of that Task.

Unless otherwise noted in the Task, the evaluator must test each item in the skills section by asking the applicant to perform each one. As safety of flight conditions permit, the evaluator may use questions during flight to test knowledge and risk management elements not evident in the demonstrated skills. To the greatest extent practicable, evaluators must test the applicant's ability to apply and correlate information, and use rote questions only when they are appropriate for the material being tested. If the Task includes an element with sub-elements, the evaluator may choose the primary element and select at least one sub-element to satisfy the requirement that at least one knowledge element be selected, For example, if the evaluator chooses IR.I.B.K3, he or she must select a sub-element like IR.I.B.K3d to satisfy the requirement to select one knowledge element.

Possible Outcomes of the Test

There are three possible outcomes of the practical test: (1) Temporary Airman Certificate (satisfactory), (2) Notice of Disapproval (unsatisfactory), or (3) Letter of Discontinuance.

If the evaluator determines that a Task is incomplete, or the outcome is uncertain, the evaluator may require the applicant to repeat that Task, or portions of that Task. This provision does not mean that instruction, practice, or the repetition of an unsatisfactory Task is permitted during the practical test.

If the evaluator determines the applicant's skill and abilities are in doubt, the outcome is unsatisfactory and the evaluator must issue a Notice of Disapproval.

Satisfactory Performance

Satisfactory performance requires that the applicant:

- demonstrate the Tasks specified in the Areas of Operation for the certificate or rating sought within the established standards;
- demonstrate mastery of the aircraft by performing each Task successfully;
- demonstrate proficiency and competency in accordance with the approved standards;
- demonstrate sound judgment and exercise aeronautical decision-making/risk management; and
- demonstrate competence in crew resource management in aircraft certificated for more than one required pilot crewmember, or single-pilot competence in an airplane that is certificated for single-pilot operations.

Satisfactory performance will result in the issuance of a temporary certificate.

Unsatisfactory Performance

Typical areas of unsatisfactory performance and grounds for disqualification include:

- Any action or lack of action by the applicant that requires corrective intervention by the evaluator to maintain safe flight.
- Failure to use proper and effective visual scanning techniques to clear the area before and while performing maneuvers.
- Consistently exceeding tolerances stated in the skill elements of the Task.
- Failure to take prompt corrective action when tolerances are exceeded.
- Failure to exercise risk management.

If, in the judgment of the evaluator, the applicant does not meet the standards for any Task, the applicant fails the Task and associated Area of Operation. The test is unsatisfactory, and the evaluator issues a Notice of Disapproval. The evaluator lists the Area(s) of Operation in which the applicant did not meet the standard, any Area(s) of Operation not tested, and the number of practical test failures. The evaluator should also list the Tasks failed or Tasks not tested within any unsatisfactory or partially completed Area(s) of Operation. If the applicant's inability to meet English language requirements contributed to the failure of a Task, the evaluator must note "English Proficiency" on the Notice of Disapproval.

The evaluator or the applicant may end the test if the applicant fails a Task. The evaluator may continue the test only with the consent of the applicant, and the applicant is entitled to credit only for those Areas of Operation and the associated Tasks performed satisfactorily.

Discontinuance

When it is necessary to discontinue a practical test for reasons other than unsatisfactory performance (e.g., equipment failure, weather, illness), the evaluator must return all test paperwork to the applicant. The evaluator must prepare, sign, and issue a Letter of Discontinuance that lists those Areas of Operation the applicant successfully completed and the date the test must be completed. The evaluator should advise the applicant to present the Letter of Discontinuance to the evaluator when the practical test resumes in order to receive credit for the items successfully completed. The Letter of Discontinuance becomes part of the applicant's certification file.

Testing after Discontinuance or Unsatisfactory Performance

To avoid having to retake the entire practical test, an applicant has 60 days from the date of a first failure or Letter of Discontinuance to pass the practical test. The evaluator's POA must include any unsatisfactory or untested Area(s) of Operation and Task(s) as indicated on the current Notice of Disapproval or Letter of Discontinuance. While an applicant may receive credit for any Task(s) successfully completed within a failed or partially tested Area of Operation, the evaluator has discretion to reevaluate any Task(s).

Practical Test Checklist (Applicant)
Appointment with Evaluator

Evaluator's Name: _____

Location: _____

Date/Time: _____

Acceptable Aircraft

- ☐ Aircraft Documents:
  - ☐ Airworthiness Certificate
  - ☐ Registration Certificate
  - ☐ Operating Limitations
- ☐ Aircraft Maintenance Records:
  - ☐ Logbook Record of Airworthiness Inspections and AD Compliance
- ☐ Pilot's Operating Handbook, FAA-Approved Aircraft Flight Manual

Personal Equipment

- ☐ View-Limiting Device
- ☐ Current Aeronautical Charts (May be electronic)
- ☐ Computer and Plotter
- ☐ Flight Plan Form
- ☐ Flight Plan Form and Flight Logs (printed or electronic)
- ☐ Chart Supplements, Airport Diagrams and Appropriate Publications (regulations, AIM, etc.)

Personal Records

- ☐ Identification—Photo/Signature ID
- ☐ Pilot Certificate
- ☐ Current Medical Certificate or BasicMed qualification
- ☐ Completed FAA Form 8710-1, Airman Certificate and/or Rating Application with Instructor's Signature or completed IACRA form
- ☐ Original Airman Knowledge Test Report
- ☐ Pilot Logbook with appropriate Instructor Endorsements
- ☐ FAA Form 8060-5, Notice of Disapproval (if applicable)
- ☐ Letter of Discontinuance (if applicable)
- ☐ Approved School Graduation Certificate (if applicable)
- ☐ Evaluator's Fee (if applicable)

Instrument Proficiency Check

14 CFR part 61, section 61.57(d) sets forth the requirements for an instrument proficiency check (IPC). Instructors and evaluators conducting an IPC must ensure the pilot meets the standards established in this ACS. A representative number of Tasks must be selected to assure the competence of the applicant to operate in the IFR environment. As a minimum, the applicant must demonstrate the ability to perform the Tasks listed in the table below. The person giving the check should develop a scenario that incorporates as many required Tasks as practical to assess the pilot's ADM and risk management skills.

Guidance on how to conduct an IPC is found in Advisory Circular 61-98, *Currency Requirements and Guidance for the Flight Review and Instrument Proficiency Check.* You may obtain a copy at www.faa.gov.

Area of Operation	IPC (Proficiency Check)[2]
I	None
II	None
III	B
IV	B
V	A
VI	All
VII[3]	B, C, D
VIII	All

---

[2] AATDs can be utilized for the majority of the IPC as specified in the Letter of Authorization issued for the device. However, the circling approach, the landing Task, and the multiengine airplane Tasks must be accomplished in an aircraft or FFS (Level B, C, or D). A BATD cannot be used for any part of the IPC.

[3] Tasks B and C are applicable only to multiengine airplanes.

Appendix 6: Safety of Flight

General

Safety of flight must be the prime consideration at all times. The evaluator, applicant, and crew must be constantly alert for other traffic. If performing aspects of a given maneuver, such as emergency procedures, would jeopardize safety, the evaluator will ask the applicant to simulate that portion of the maneuver. The evaluator will assess the applicant's use of visual scanning and collision avoidance procedures throughout the entire test.

Stall and Spin Awareness

During flight training and testing, the applicant and the instructor or evaluator must always recognize and avoid operations that could lead to an inadvertent stall or spin.

Use of Checklists

Throughout the practical test, the applicant is evaluated on the use of an appropriate checklist.

Assessing proper checklist use depends upon the specific Task. In all cases, the evaluator should determine whether the applicant appropriately divides attention and uses proper visual scanning. In some situations, reading the actual checklist may be impractical or unsafe. In such cases, the evaluator should assess the applicant's performance of published or recommended immediate action "memory" items along with his or her review of the appropriate checklist once conditions permit.

In a single-pilot airplane, the applicant should demonstrate the crew resource management (CRM) principles described as single-pilot resource management (SRM). Proper use is dependent on the specific Task being evaluated. The situation may be such that the use of the checklist while accomplishing elements of an Objective would be either unsafe or impractical in a single-pilot operation. In this case, a review of the checklist after the elements have been accomplished is appropriate. Use of a checklist should also consider visual scanning and division of attention at all times.

Use of Distractions

Numerous studies indicate that many accidents have occurred when the pilot has been distracted during critical phases of flight. The evaluator should incorporate realistic distractions during the flight portion of the practical test to evaluate the pilot's situational awareness and ability to utilize proper control technique while dividing attention both inside and outside the flight deck.

Positive Exchange of Flight Controls

There must always be a clear understanding of who has control of the aircraft. Prior to flight, the pilots involved should conduct a briefing that includes reviewing the procedures for exchanging flight controls.

The FAA recommends a positive three-step process for exchanging flight controls between pilots:

- When one pilot seeks to have the other pilot take control of the aircraft, he or she will say, "You have the flight controls."
- The second pilot acknowledges immediately by saying, "I have the flight controls."
- The first pilot again says, "You have the flight controls," and visually confirms the exchange.

Pilots should follow this procedure during any exchange of flight controls, including any occurrence during the practical test. The FAA also recommends that both pilots use a visual check to verify that the exchange has occurred. There must never be any doubt as to who is flying the aircraft.

Aeronautical Decision-Making, Risk Management, Crew Resource Management and Single-Pilot Resource Management

Throughout the practical test, the evaluator must assess the applicant's ability to use sound aeronautical decision-making procedures in order to identify hazards and mitigate risk. The evaluator must accomplish this requirement by reference to the risk management elements of the given Task(s), and by developing scenarios that incorporate and combine Tasks appropriate to assessing the applicant's risk management in making safe aeronautical decisions. For example, the evaluator may develop a scenario that incorporates weather decisions and performance planning.

In assessing the applicant's performance, the evaluator should take note of the applicant's use of CRM and, if appropriate, SRM. CRM/SRM is the set of competencies that includes situational awareness, communication skills, teamwork, task allocation, and decision-making within a comprehensive framework of standard operating procedures (SOP). SRM specifically refers to the management of all resources onboard the aircraft as well as outside resources available to the single pilot.

Deficiencies in CRM/SRM almost always contribute to the unsatisfactory performance of a Task. While evaluation of CRM/SRM may appear to be somewhat subjective, the evaluator should use the risk management elements of the given Task(s) to determine whether the applicant's performance of the Task(s) demonstrates both understanding and application of the associated risk management elements.

Multiengine Considerations

For multiengine practical tests conducted in the airplane, the evaluator must discuss with the applicant during the required preflight briefing the methods for simulating an engine failure in accordance with the aircraft manufacturer's recommended procedures.

Practical tests conducted in an FSTD can only be accomplished as part of an approved curriculum or training program. Any limitations for powerplant failure will be noted in that program.

Appendix 7: Aircraft, Equipment, and Operational Requirements & Limitations

Aircraft Requirements & Limitations

14 CFR part 61, section 61.45 prescribes the required aircraft and equipment for a practical test. The regulation states the minimum aircraft registration and airworthiness requirements as well as the minimum equipment requirements, to include the minimum required controls.

Applicants testing in a multiengine airplane must provide a multiengine airplane with a published V_{MC}. The only exception is if the airman's certificate is limited to center thrust. If the aircraft presented for the practical test has inoperative instruments or equipment, it must be addressed in accordance with 14 CFR part 91, section 91.213. If the aircraft can be operated in accordance with 14 CFR part 91, section 91.213, then it must be determined if the inoperative instruments or equipment are required to complete the practical test.

Equipment Requirements & Limitations

The equipment examination should be administered before the flight portion of the practical test, but it must be closely coordinated and related to the flight portion. In a training core curriculum that has been approved under 14 CFR part 142, the evaluator may accept written evidence of the equipment exam, provided that the Administrator has approved the exam and authorized the individual who administers it. This section requires the aircraft must:

- Be of U.S., foreign, or military registry of the same category, class and type, if applicable, for the certificate and/or rating for which the applicant is applying.

- Have fully functional dual controls, except as provided for in 14 CFR part 61, section, 61.45 (c) and (e); and

- Be capable of performing all Areas of Operation appropriate to the rating sought and have no operating limitations, which prohibit its use in any of the Area of Operation, required for the practical test.

Consistent with 14 CFR part 61, section 61.45 (b) and (d), the aircraft must have:

- the flight instruments necessary for controlling the aircraft without outside references,
- the radio equipment required for ATC communications, and
- the ability to perform instrument approach procedures
- GPS equipment must be instrument certified and contain the current database.

To assist in management of the aircraft during the practical test, the applicant is expected to demonstrate automation management skills by utilizing installed equipment such as autopilot, avionics and systems displays, and/or a flight management system (FMS). The evaluator is expected to test the applicant's knowledge of the systems that are installed and operative during both the oral and flight portions of the practical test. If the applicant has trained using a class 1 or class 2 EFB to display charts and data, and wishes to use the EFB during the practical test, the applicant is expected to demonstrate appropriate knowledge, risk management, and skill.

If the practical test is conducted in an aircraft, the applicant is required by 14 CFR part 61, section 61.45(d)(2) to provide an appropriate view limiting device acceptable to the evaluator. The applicant and the evaluator should establish a procedure as to when and how this device should be donned and removed, and brief this procedure before the flight. The device must be used during all testing that has flight "solely by reference to instruments" included as part of the Task objective. This device must prevent the applicant from having visual reference outside the aircraft, but it must not restrict the evaluator's ability to see and avoid other traffic. The use of the device does not apply to specific elements within a Task when there is a requirement for visual references.

Operational Requirements, Limitations, & Task Information

V. Navigation Systems

While the applicant is expected to be able to fly DME Arcs, they may be selected for testing only if they are charted and available.

VI. Instrument Approach Procedures

Stabilized Approach Criteria

A stabilized approach is characterized by a constant angle, constant rate of descent approach profile ending near the touchdown point, where the landing maneuver begins.

Use of RNAV or GPS System

If the practical test is conducted in an airplane equipped with an approach-approved RNAV or GPS system or FSTD that is equipped to replicate an approved RNAV or GPS system, the applicant must demonstrate approach proficiency using that system. If the applicant has contracted for training in an approved course that includes GPS training, and the airplane/FSTD has a properly installed and operable GPS, the applicant must demonstrate GPS approach proficiency.

Localizer Performance with Vertical Guidance (LPV Minimums)

Localizer performance with vertical guidance (LPV) minimums with a decision altitude (DA) greater than 300 feet height above touchdown (HAT) may be used as a nonprecision approach; however, due to the precision of its glidepath and localizer-like lateral navigation characteristics, an LPV minimums approach can be used to demonstrate precision approach proficiency if the DA is equal to or less than 300 feet HAT.

Vertical or Lateral Deviation Standard

The standard is to allow no more than a ¾ scale deflection of either the vertical or lateral deviation indications during the final approach. As markings on flight instruments vary, a ¾ scale deflection of either vertical or lateral guidance is deemed to occur when it is displaced three-fourths of the distance that it may be deflected from the indication representing that the aircraft is on the correct flight path.

Task A. Nonprecision Approach

The evaluator will select nonprecision approaches representative of the type that the applicant is likely to use. The choices must use at least two different types of navigational aids.

Examples of acceptable nonprecision approaches include: VOR, VOR/DME, LOC procedures on an ILS, LDA, RNAV (RNP) or RNAV (GPS) to LNAV, LNAV/VNAV or LPV line of minima as long as the LPV DA is greater than 300 feet HAT. The equipment must be installed and the database must be current and qualified to fly GPS-based approaches.

The applicant must accomplish at least two nonprecision approaches in simulated or actual weather conditions.

- One must include a procedure turn or, in the case of a GPS-based approach, a Terminal Arrival Area (TAA) procedure.
- At least one must be flown without the use of autopilot and without the assistance of radar vectors. The yaw damper and flight director are not considered parts of the autopilot for purposes of this Task.
- One is expected to be flown with reference to backup or partial panel instrumentation or navigation display, depending on the aircraft's instrument avionics configuration, representing the failure mode(s) most realistic for the equipment used.

The evaluator has discretion to have the applicant perform a landing or a missed approach at the completion of each non precision approach.

Task B. Precision Approach

The applicant must accomplish a precision approach to the decision altitude (DA) using aircraft navigational equipment for centerline and vertical guidance in simulated or actual instrument conditions. Acceptable instrument approaches for this part of the practical test are the ILS and GLS. In addition, if the installed equipment and database is current and qualified for IFR flight and approaches to LPV minima, an LPV minima approach can be flown to demonstrate precision approach proficiency if the LPV DA is equal to or less than 300 feet HAT.

The evaluator has discretion to have the applicant perform a landing or a missed approach at the completion of the precision approach.

Appendix 8: Use of Flight Simulation Training Devices (FSTD) and Aviation Training Devices (ATD): Airplane Single-Engine, Multiengine Land and Sea

Use of Flight Simulator Training Devices

14 CFR part 61, section 61.4, *Qualification and approval of flight simulators and flight training devices*, states in paragraph (a) that each full flight simulator (FFS) and flight training device (FTD) used for training, and for which an airman is to receive credit to satisfy any training, testing, or checking requirement under this chapter, must be qualified and approved by the Administrator for—

(1) the training, testing, and checking for which it is used;

(2) each particular maneuver, procedure, or crewmember function performed; and

(3) the representation of the specific category and class of aircraft, type of aircraft, particular variation within the type of aircraft, or set of aircraft for certain flight training devices.

14 CFR part 60 prescribes the rules governing the initial and continuing qualification and use of all Flight Simulator Training Devices (FSTD) used for meeting training, evaluation, or flight experience requirements for flight crewmember certification or qualification.

An FSTD is defined in 14 CFR part 60 as an FFS or FTD:

Full Flight Simulator (FFS)—a replica of a specific type, make, model, or series aircraft. It includes the equipment and computer programs necessary to represent aircraft operations in ground and flight conditions, a visual system providing an out-of-the-flight deck view, a system that provides cues at least equivalent to those of a three-degree-of-freedom motion system, and has the full range of capabilities of the systems installed in the device as described in part 60 of this chapter and the qualification performance standard (QPS) for a specific FFS qualification level. (part 1)

Flight Training Device (FTD)—a replica of aircraft instruments, equipment, panels, and controls in an open flight deck area or an enclosed aircraft flight deck replica. It includes the equipment and computer programs necessary to represent aircraft (or set of aircraft) operations in ground and flight conditions having the full range of capabilities of the systems installed in the device as described in part 60 of this chapter and the QPS for a specific FTD qualification level. (part 1)

The FAA National Simulator Program (NSP) qualifies Level A-D FFSs and Level 4 – 7[4] FTDs. In addition, each operational rule part identifies additional requirements for the approval and use of FSTDs in a training program[5]. Use of an FSTD for the completion of the instrument-airplane rating practical test is permitted only when accomplished in accordance with an FAA approved curriculum or training program. Use of an FSTD for the completion of an instrument proficiency check is also permitted when accomplished in accordance with an FAA approved curriculum or training program.

---

[4] The FSTD qualification standards in effect prior to part 60 defined a Level 7 FTD for airplanes (see Advisory Circular 120-45A, Airplane Flight Training Device Qualification, 1992). This device required high fidelity, airplane specific aerodynamic and flight control models similar to a Level D FFS, but did not require a motion cueing system or visual display system. In accordance with the "grandfather rights" of 14 CFR part 60, section 60.17, these previously qualified devices will retain their qualification basis as long as they continue to meet the standards under which they were originally qualified. There is only one airplane Level 7 FTD with grandfather rights that remains in the U.S. As a result of changes to part 60 that were published in the Federal Register in March 2016, the airplane Level 7 FTD was reinstated with updated evaluation standards. The new Level 7 FTD will require a visual display system for qualification. The minimum qualified Tasks for the Level 7 FTD are described in Table B1B of Appendix B of part 60.

[5] 14 CFR part 121, section 121.407; part 135, section 135.335; part 141, section 141.41; and part 142, section 142.59.

Use of Aviation Training Devices

14 CFR part 61, section 61.4(c) states the Administrator may approve a device other than an FFS or FTD for specific purposes. Under this authority, the FAA's General Aviation and Commercial Division provides approvals for aviation training devices (ATD).

Advisory Circular (AC) 61-136A, *FAA Approval of Aviation Training Devices and Their Use for Training and Experience,* provides information and guidance for the required function, performance, and effective use of ATDs for pilot training and aeronautical experience (including instrument currency). FAA issues a letter of authorization (LOA) to an ATD manufacturer approving an ATD as a basic aviation training device (BATD) or an advanced aviation training device (AATD). LOAs are valid for a five year period with a specific expiration date and include the amount of credit a pilot may take for training and experience requirements.

> *Aviation Training Device (ATD)—a training device, other than an FFS or FTD, that has been evaluated, qualified, and approved by the Administrator. In general, this includes a replica of aircraft instruments, equipment, panels, and controls in an open flight deck area or an enclosed aircraft cockpit. It includes the hardware and software necessary to represent a category and class of aircraft (or set of aircraft) operations in ground and flight conditions having the appropriate range of capabilities and systems installed in the device as described within the AC 61-136 for the specific basic or advanced qualification level.*

> *Basic Aviation Training Device (BATD)—provides an adequate training platform for both procedural and operational performance Tasks specific to instrument experience and the ground and flight training requirements for the Private Pilot Certificate and instrument rating per 14 CFR parts 61 and 141.*

> *Advanced Aviation Training Device (AATD)—provides an adequate training platform for both procedural and operational performance Tasks specific to the ground and flight training requirements for the Private Pilot Certificate, Instrument Rating, Commercial Pilot Certificate, Airline Transport Pilot (ATP) Certificate, and Flight Instructor Certificate per 14 CFR parts 61 and 141. It also provides an adequate platform for Tasks required for instrument experience and the instrument proficiency check.*

Note: ATDs cannot be used for practical tests, aircraft type specific training, or for an aircraft type rating; therefore the use of an ATD for the instrument – airplane rating practical test is not permitted. An AATD, however, may be used for some of the required Tasks of an instrument proficiency check as further explained in this appendix.

Credit for Time in an FSTD

14 CFR part 61, section 61.65 specifies the minimum aeronautical experience requirements for a person applying for an instrument rating. Paragraph (d) specifies the time requirements for an instrument-airplane rating, which includes specific experience requirements that must be completed in an airplane. Paragraph (h) of this section specifies the amount of credit a pilot can take for time in an FFS or FTD. For those that received training in programs outside of 14 CFR part 142, section 61.65(h)(2)[6] applies. For those pilots that received training through a 14 CFR part 142 program, section 61.65(h)(1) applies.

Credit for Time in an ATD

14 CFR part 61, section 61.65 specifies the minimum aeronautical experience requirements for a person applying for an instrument rating. Paragraph (d) specifies the time requirements for an instrument-airplane rating, which includes specific experience requirements that must be completed in an airplane. Paragraph (i) specifies the maximum instrument time in an ATD a pilot may credit towards the instrument rating aeronautical experience requirements. Paragraph (j) specifies the maximum instrument time a pilot may credit in any combination of an FFS, FTD, and ATD.

In order to credit pilot time, the ATD must be FAA-approved and the instrument time must be provided by an authorized instructor. AC 61-136A, states the LOA for each approved ATD will indicate the credit allowances for pilot training and experience, as provided under 14 CFR parts 61 and 141. Time with an instructor in a BATD and an AATD may be credited towards the aeronautical experience requirements for the instrument-airplane rating as specified in the LOA for the device used. It is recommended that applicants who intend to take credit for time in a

---

[6] As part of program approval, 14 CFR part 141 training providers must also adhere to the requirements for permitted time in an FFS, FTD, or ATD per Appendix C to 14 CFR part 141.

BATD or an AATD towards the aeronautical experience requirements for the instrument-airplane rating obtain a copy of the LOA for each device used so they have a record for how much credit may be taken. For additional information on the logging of ATD time, reference Appendix 4 of AC 61-136.

Instrument Experience

14 CFR part 61, section 61.57 provides the recent flight experience requirements to serve as a PIC. Paragraph (c) specifies the necessary instrument experience required to serve as a PIC under IFR. The experience may be gained in an airplane, an FSTD, or an ATD. Refer to the subparagraphs of 14 CFR part 61, section 61.57(c) to determine the experience needed.

Instrument Proficiency Check

If a person fails to meet the experience requirements of 14 CFR part 61, section 61.57(c), a pilot may only establish instrument currency through an instrument proficiency check as described in 14 CFR section 61.57(d). An FSTD may be used as part of an approved curriculum to accomplish all or portions of this check. If specified in its LOA, an AATD may be used to complete most of the required Tasks. However, the circling approach, the landing Task, and the multiengine airplane Tasks must be accomplished in an aircraft or FFS (Level B, C, or D). A BATD cannot be used for an instrument proficiency check. See the Instrument Proficiency Check table in Appendix 5: Practical Test Roles, Responsibilities, and Outcomes for additional information.

Use of an FSTD on a Practical Test

14 CFR part 61, section 61.45 specifies the required aircraft and equipment that must be provided for a practical test unless permitted to use an FFS or FTD for the flight portion. 14 CFR part 61, section 61 64 provides the criteria for using an FSTD for a practical test. Specifically, paragraph (a) states –

> If an applicant for a certificate or rating uses a flight simulator or flight training device for training or any portion of the practical test, the flight simulator and flight training device—
>
> > (1) Must represent the category, class, and type (if a type rating is applicable) for the rating sought; and
> >
> > (2) Must be qualified and approved by the Administrator and used in accordance with an approved course of training under 14 CFR part 141 or 142 of this chapter; or under 14 CFR part 121 or part 135 of this chapter, provided the applicant is a pilot employee of that air carrier operator.

Therefore, practical tests or portions thereof, when accomplished in an FSTD, may only be conducted by FAA aviation safety inspectors (ASI), aircrew program designees (APD) authorized to conduct such tests in FSTDs in 14 CFR parts 121 or 135, qualified personnel and designees authorized to conduct such tests in FSTDs for 14 CFR part 141 pilot school graduates, or appropriately authorized 14 CFR part 142 Training Center Evaluators (TCE).

In addition, 14 CFR part 61, section 61.64(b) states if an airplane is not used during the practical test for a type rating for a turbojet airplane (except for preflight inspection), an applicant must accomplish the entire practical test in a Level C or higher FFS and the applicant must meet the specific experience criteria listed. If the experience criteria cannot be met, the applicant can either—

> (f)(1) [...] complete the following s on the practical test in an aircraft appropriate to category, class, and type for the rating sought: Preflight inspection, normal takeoff, normal instrument landing system approach, missed approach, and normal landing; or
>
> (f)(2) The applicant's pilot certificate will be issued with a limitation that states: "The [name of the additional type rating] is subject to pilot-in-command limitations," and the applicant is restricted from serving as pilot-in-command in an aircraft of that type.

When flight Tasks are accomplished in an airplane, certain Task elements may be accomplished through "simulated" actions in the interest of safety and practicality. However, when accomplished in an FFS or FTD, these same actions would not be "simulated." For example, when in an airplane, a simulated engine fire may be addressed by retarding the throttle to idle, simulating the shutdown of the engine, simulating the discharge of the fire suppression agent, if applicable, and simulating the disconnection of associated electrical, hydraulic, and pneumatics systems. However, when the same emergency condition is addressed in an FSTD, all Task elements must be accomplished as would be expected under actual circumstances.

Similarly, safety of flight precautions taken in the airplane for the accomplishment of a specific maneuver or procedure (such as limiting altitude in an approach to stall or setting maximum airspeed for an engine failure expected to result in a rejected takeoff) need not be taken when an FSTD is used. It is important to understand that, whether accomplished in an airplane or FSTD, all Tasks and elements for each maneuver or procedure must have the same performance standards applied equally for determination of overall satisfactory performance.

Appendix 9: References

This ACS is based on the following 14 CFR parts, FAA guidance documents, manufacturer's publications, and other documents.

Reference	Title
14 CFR part 61	Certification: Pilots, Flight Instructors, and Ground Instructors
14 CFR part 68	Requirements for Operating Certain Small Aircraft Without a Medical Certificate
14 CFR part 91	General Operating and Flight Rules
AC 00-6	Aviation Weather
AC 00-45	Aviation Weather Services
AC 60-28	English Language Skill Standards Required by 14 CFR parts 61, 63 and 65
AC 61-136	FAA Approval of Aviation Training Devices and Their Use for Training and Experience
AC 68-1	Alternative Pilot Physical Examination and Education Requirements
AC 91-74	Pilot Guide: Flight in Icing Conditions
AC 91.21-1	Use of Portable Electronic Devices Aboard Aircraft
AC 120-108	Continuous Descent Final Approach
AFM	Airplane Flight Manual
AIM	Aeronautical Information Manual
FAA-H-8083-2	Risk Management Handbook
FAA-H-8083-3	Airplane Flying Handbook
FAA-H-8083-15	Instrument Flying Handbook
FAA-H-8083-16	Instrument Procedures Handbook
FAA-H-8083-25	Pilot's Handbook of Aeronautical Knowledge
IFP	Instrument Flight Procedures
POH/AFM	Pilot's Operating Handbook/FAA-Approved Airplane Flight Manual
Other	Chart Supplements
	Navigation Charts
	NOTAMs

Note: *Users should reference the current edition of the reference documents listed above. The current edition of all FAA publications can be found at www.faa.gov.*

Appendix 10: Abbreviations and Acronyms

The following abbreviations and acronyms are used in the ACS.

Abb./Acronym	Definition
14 CFR	Title 14 of the Code of Federal Regulations
AATD	Advanced Aviation Training Device
AC	Advisory Circular
ACS	Airman Certification Standards
ADM	Aeronautical Decision-Making
AELS	Aviation English Language Standard
AFM	Airplane Flight Manual
AFS	Flight Standards Service
AIM	Aeronautical Information Manual
AKTR	Airman Knowledge Test Report
AMEL	Airplane Multiengine Land
AMES	Airplane Multiengine Sea
AOO	Area of Operation
ASEL	Airplane Single-Engine Land
ASES	Airplane Single-Engine Sea
ASI	Aviation Safety Inspector
ATC	Air Traffic Control
ATD	Aviation Training Device
ATP	Airline Transport Pilot
BATD	Basic Aviation Training Device
CDFA	Constant Descent Final Approach
CDI	Course Deviation Indicator
CFIT	Controlled Flight Into Terrain
CFR	Code of Federal Regulations
CRM	Crew Resource Management
DA	Decision Altitude
DH	Decision Height
DME	Distance Measuring Equipment
DP	Departure Procedures
DPE	Designated Pilot Examiner
FAA	Federal Aviation Administration
FFS	Full Flight Simulator
FMS	Flight Management System
FSDO	Flight Standards District Office
FSTD	Flight Simulation Training Device
FTD	Flight Training Device
GPS	Global Positioning System
HAT	Height Above Threshold (Touchdown)
IACRA	Integrated Airman Certificate and Rating Application
ICAO	International Civil Aviation Organization
IFO	International Field Office
IFP	Instrument Flight Procedures
IFR	Instrument Flight Rules

Abb./Acronym	Definition
IFU	International Field Unit
ILS	Instrument Landing System
IMC	Instrument Meteorological Conditions
ICP	Instrument Rating Airplane *Canadian Conversion*
IPC	Instrument Proficiency Check
IR	Instrument Rating
IRA	Instrument Rating Airplane
LDA	Localizer-Type Directional Aid
LOA	Letter of Authorization
LOC	ILS Localizer
LPV	Localizer Performance with Vertical Guidance
LSC	Learning Statement Codes
MAP	Missed Approach Point
MDA	Minimum Descent Altitude
MFD	Multi-function Display
NAS	National Airspace System
NOTAMs	Notices to Airmen
NSP	National Simulator Program
PAR	Private Pilot Airplane
PFD	Primary Flight Display
PIC	Pilot-in-Command
POA	Plan of Action
POH	Pilot's Operating Handbook
QPS	Qualification Performance Standard
RAIM	Receiver Autonomous Integrity Monitoring
RNAV	Area Navigation
RNP	Required Navigation Performance
SMS	Safety Management System
SOP	Standard Operating Procedures
SRM	Single-Pilot Resource Management
STAR	Standard Terminal Arrival
UTC	Coordinated Universal Time
VDP	Visual Descent Point
VFR	Visual Flight Rules
V_{MC}	Minimum Control Speed with the Critical Engine Inoperative
VOR	Very High Frequency Omnidirectional Range
WAAS	Wide Area Augmentation System